HOCKEY GREATS

Awesome Centres

Mike Leonetti

Scholastic Canada Ltd.

Toronto New York London Auckland Sydney
Mexico City New Delhi Hong Kong Buenos Aires

Scholastic Canada Ltd.
604 King Street West, Toronto, Ontario M5V 1E1, Canada

Scholastic Inc.
557 Broadway, New York, NY 10012, USA

Scholastic Australia Pty Limited
PO Box 579, Gosford, NSW 2250, Australia

Scholastic New Zealand Limited
Private Bag 94407, Botany, Manukau 2163, New Zealand

Scholastic Children's Books
Euston House, 24 Eversholt Street, London NW1 1DB, UK

Cover, 2, 6, 34, 46: Hockey Hall of Fame; p. 10,15: Frank Prazak/Hockey Hall of
Fame; p. 12: Hall of Fame; p. 18, 20, 26: Turofsky/Hockey Hall of Fame; p. 26, 66:
Hockey Hall of Fame; p. 31: Graphic Artists/Hockey Hall of Fame; p. 41, 61: Paul
Bereswill/Hockey Hall of Fame; p. 46: Walter Gretzky/Hockey Hall of Fame; p. 51:
© Sun Media; p. 55: Robert Shaver/Hockey Hall of Fame; p. 64: Doug MacLellan/
Hockey Hall of Fame; p: 69: Dave Sandford/Hockey Hall of Fame; p. 78: Dave
Sandford/Getty Images; p. 81: Brian Bahr/Getty Images; p. 85: Hockey Hall of Fame;
p. 90, 100: Matthew Manor/Hockey Hall of Fame; p. 95: Walt Neubrand/Hockey
Hall of Fame; p. 103: All Children's Hospital, Florida; p. 107: © Getty Images; Centre
ice illustration: © Fejas/Shutterstock; Player silhouette © dusan.dada/Shutterstock

Library and Archives Canada Cataloguing in Publication

Leonetti, Mike, 1958-
Awesome centres / Mike Leonetti.

(Hockey greats)
ISBN 978-0-545-98689-2

1. Hockey players--Biography--Juvenile literature. 2. National Hockey
League--Biography--Juvenile literature. I. Title. II. Series: Hockey greats

GV848.5.A1L45 2010   j796.962092'2   C2010-901939-3

6 5 4 3 2 1   Printed in Canada 119   10 11 12 13 14

TABLE OF CONTENTS

INTRODUCTION

A winning hockey team is made up of many parts: great goaltending, defencemen who can move the puck, and good forwards who can score goals. The most important of the forwards are the players who play the centre ice position. A top centre is the heart of any great forward line. And there were none better than Jean Béliveau, Wayne Gretzky and Vincent Lecavalier — the three players profiled in this book. Each player led his team to the Stanley Cup.

Béliveau had a special role as captain of the Montreal Canadiens. He played with the Habs when the team was very important to so many people in Quebec — especially to French Canadians. Béliveau first joined the Canadiens in the early 1950s and learned to win and lead by playing with other stars like Maurice "Rocket" Richard. When it was time for Béliveau to lead the team, he was ready for the job, and he did it well. Montreal won the Cup a total of five times with Béliveau as captain. He ended a Hall of Fame career with a final championship in 1971. He has remained a part of the Canadiens team since he retired, and all hockey fans who watched him play recall how graciously number 4 conducted himself both on and off the ice. He is still revered whenever he attends a Montreal Canadiens game today.

Gretzky was a young man who loved the game of hockey more than anything. He was dedicated to being the best player possible. He started his great Canadian dream of playing in the NHL with a rink in the backyard of his own home! Before his career was over, Gretzky had broken almost every record in the NHL. He also won the Stanley Cup four times and was the most valuable player in the NHL a total of nine times. In addition to all his records, "The Great One" is looked upon as one of the best athletes in all of sports. Gretzky learned a lot about how a captain should act by watching Béliveau on *Hockey Night in Canada*. Gretzky was chosen to light the flame to open the 2010 Winter Olympic Games in Vancouver because he means so much to all of Canada.

Lecavalier was selected by the worst team in the NHL when the Tampa Bay Lightning took him as the first pick of the 1998 draft. It wasn't easy for young Lecavalier in the early years of his career, but he didn't give up. Eventually the Lightning got better, and Lecavalier became the most talented forward on the team. He was at his best when the club won the Stanley Cup in 2004, defeating the Calgary Flames in seven games. He also played an important role when Canada won the first World Cup of Hockey in 2004. He scored a league-best 52 goals in 2006–07. As captain of the Lightning, he still has many more great moments ahead of him.

Great players like Béliveau, Gretzky and Lecavalier produced memorable moments, many of them captured in this book. There is much to be learned from watching as the best do their work. These three players are fine examples of how great the sport of hockey has been over many years. There is no finer trio of stars to show how hard work, determination and leadership can lead to success. Enjoy their interesting stories!

JEAN BÉLIVEAU

THE FIRST WINNER OF THE CONN SMYTHE TROPHY

"This is it, the seventh and deciding game. The winner gets the Stanley Cup," said legendary broadcaster Danny Gallivan as the *Hockey Night in Canada* broadcast began on the night of May 1, 1965. The Montreal Canadiens were at home to the Chicago Black Hawks and were favoured to win, since the entire series to date had seen the home team win each game. The pressure was on Montreal — they had not won the championship in five years, and all the Canadiens were anxious to bring the Cup back home. A lot was expected from team captain Jean Béliveau. He had won five titles already, but none as the Habs' leader. Would tonight be the night he would lift the famous trophy for the first time as captain?

The Montreal crowd was nervous as the game began, but seconds after the puck was dropped, the Canadiens swarmed into the Chicago end. Béliveau, with teammates

Bobby Rousseau and Dick Duff, went on the attack and forced a turnover. Rousseau's shot hit Béliveau before bouncing past the startled Black Hawk goalie Glenn Hall into the net, and a big smile came to the face of the Montreal captain.

A little while later, Béliveau set up Duff with a perfect pass to make it 2–0 for Montreal. The Canadiens knew they had the Black Hawks on the run. Montreal netminder Gump Worsley was having no trouble handling the Chicago attack, which featured stars like Bobby Hull and Stan Mikita. A penalty to defenceman Pierre Pilote gave Montreal a late power play and the speedy Yvan Cournoyer capitalized on it, bringing the score to 3–0. Henri Richard made it 4–0 before the first period was over, on another powerplay opportunity. Chicago could do little the rest of the way, as Montreal coasted to an easy win.

Béliveau took the last faceoff of the game and the crowd chanted down the final seconds. He lifted his stick as the siren went off and galloped down the ice to where the Canadiens were mobbing Worsley. He handed his stick to a boy who found his way onto the ice during the celebration, then skated over to the table where the Stanley Cup was sitting and lifted the Cup for the first time as captain.

The star centre addressed the crowd in both French and English. "It's a great pleasure for me to express, on behalf of all my teammates and all members of the Canadiens, how pleased we are to win the Stanley Cup not only for us but for all of you, our great supporters." He then took the Cup and skated around the ice with it, posing for photos.

But this was not Béliveau's only honour. He was also the first winner of the new Conn Smythe Trophy for the best player in the playoffs. "It is certainly nice to win this beautiful trophy, but I want to thank all my teammates," he said graciously.

Conn Smythe himself offered his opinion on the Montreal centre: "Jean Béliveau is the best thing that has happened to modern hockey."

Béliveau (with microphone) after his Stanley Cup win in 1968. Béliveau with the Cup soon became a familiar image to Montreal fans.

GROWING UP IN QUEBEC

When his first-born son, Jean, came into the world on August 31, 1931, Arthur Béliveau knew that his son's world was going to be much different than his own. Still, he was determined to instill in young Jean a deep respect for religion, hard work and self discipline.

Arthur and his wife Laurette had settled in the town of Victoriaville to raise their family of seven: five boys and two girls. There, Jean played shinny in the backyard. He learned to handle the puck with ease on the crowded ice and would skate all day long on the weekends. His mother would put cardboard on the floor of the house when it was time for lunch so that the boys wouldn't have to remove their skates. Jean also played at the rink next to his school, where the tall, skinny kid with the blue toque would go up against boys of all ages — many of them bigger and older. He had developed the muscles

Béliveau played with the Victoriaville Tigers from 1947 to 1949.

that would help him to compete against the older boys by helping his father cut down broken hydro poles that he got from work, for firewood.

Béliveau did not play on an organized team until he was 12 years old. But by the time he was 16, he'd scored 46 goals in 42 games for his new team, the Victoriaville Tigers of the Quebec Junior Hockey League, and people were beginning to take notice of the young man.

Béliveau was also a good baseball player, but it was his hockey prowess that got him noticed all across the province. His father never really wanted his son to become a hockey player. He would have preferred that Béliveau work with him at Shawinigan Light and Power, but he soon became convinced that hockey was going to make Jean wealthy and famous.

Béliveau sat around the radio with his family during the 1944–45 season, listening to Canadiens games as his idol Maurice "Rocket" Richard scored 50 goals in 50 games and Montreal won the Stanley Cup. He dreamed of playing for the Canadiens as well one day, and of holding the big trophy. After a second great season with Victoriaville (a league-leading 48 goals in 42 games), Béliveau headed to Quebec City to play for the Citadelles. In December of 1949, his father saw him off to the bus to Quebec City and told him simply, "Do your best, Jean."

It was an exciting time for the Citadelles, who now

had the best young player in Canada on their squad, as well as a brand-new arena. Béliveau scored 38 goals in his first season and 61 during the 1950–51 campaign. He also added 63 assists for a league-leading total of 124 points. That same season the young Béliveau stepped up to play in one game for the Quebec Aces in a senior league, scoring two goals, and two games with the Montreal Canadiens, where he earned one goal and one assist.

The Canadiens were very anxious to sign the young superstar now that his junior career was over, but Béliveau felt a strong loyalty to those in Quebec City who had been very generous to him in so many ways. He was given a new car one year, and whenever he scored a hat trick, a suit and a pair of socks would be given to him. He got so many he started giving them away to teammates! He decided to stay two more seasons in Quebec City to play senior hockey, knowing that the Aces would pay him as much as an NHL team, and with the knowledge that the Canadiens would still be there later.

Canadiens management was very disappointed with Béliveau's decision. They wanted to add him to their other young stars like Bernie Geoffrion, Dickie Moore and Jacques Plante who, they felt, were going to take over as the team's new leaders.

Playing for the Aces gave Béliveau a chance to learn from older players and more time to prepare for the NHL.

Béliveau with the Quebec Aces

He was coached by Punch Imlach (who would go on to great success with the Toronto Maple Leafs in the 1960s) who thought Béliveau was the best player he had ever seen. Imlach helped Béliveau improve his skating, a vital skill for NHL success. Béliveau made the most of his time in Quebec, leading the Quebec Senior Hockey League in goal-scoring both seasons (45 goals in 1951–52 and 50 in 1952–53). He was also the top point producer each year (83 and 89 points respectively). The 1952–53 season also saw Béliveau play in five games for the Canadiens, where he scored five times, including his first NHL hat trick.

Attendance at the Quebec Coliseum — "The House that Jean Built" — reached the 360,000 mark in Béliveau's last season with the Aces, with most fans there to watch the superbly talented centre. At this point Béliveau had done all he could in Quebec City, including delivering a championship. Now nicknamed "Le Gros Bill" by a newspaper writer, after the title of a French Canadian song which started with the line "Here Comes Big Bill," Béliveau knew his ultimate calling was in Montreal, where he would finally put on the famous red, white and blue sweater. The 22-year-old star decided it was time to make a move to the big city.

THE GREATEST TEAM IN HOCKEY HISTORY

The Montreal Canadiens had tried to sign Jean Béliveau before, but he had turned them down until he felt his obligations to Quebec City were done. Montreal general manager Frank Selke was under a lot of pressure to sign Béliveau, but he had always been careful not to push too hard. By October of 1953, the Stanley Cup champions felt they had no choice but to pursue Béliveau and get his name on a contract. Even though Montreal had won the championship, leading centre Elmer Lach was not far away from retirement and the Habs knew they needed to groom a replacement quickly.

Just before the 1953–54 season was to begin, Selke said that he "opened up the vault and said, 'help yourself, Jean!'" In the end the young French Canadian centre signed a five-year deal worth a total of $100,000 — an unheard of amount in those days. Yet it was all worth it

Béliveau heads to the ice.

for the Habs, who now had a new superstar locked up. And their fans were ecstatic! Béliveau decided to wear sweater number 4 since number 9 belonged to his idol, Maurice Richard. Soon number 4 would become nearly as popular as Richard's.

Béliveau's NHL career got off to a rough start. He suffered two injuries and played in just 44 games in his rookie season, scoring 13 times and totalling 34 points. He came on strong late in the season, though: on the weekend of March 13–14, 1954, he scored three goals and added two assists in games the Canadiens won 4–0 and 6–0 over the Chicago Black Hawks. The next year Béliveau scored 37 times in 70 games, ringing up a total of 73 points — just one behind Richard and two behind Geoffrion, as Montreal boasted the top three scorers in the league. But the Canadiens lost out to Detroit in the playoffs for the second season in a row.

It was the 1955–56 season where Béliveau and the Canadiens rose to the top. Montreal coach Dick Irvin felt the opposition was taking advantage of Béliveau's calm demeanor on the ice and urged him to play more aggressively. His penalty minute total went from 58 to 143 and every aspect of his game improved. The big centre, now 6'3" and 205 pounds (1.91 metres, 93 kilograms), started to play to his full capabilities and led the NHL in goals with 47 and in points with 88. He showed his excellent playmaking skills and an ability to finish plays in close,

Béliveau (right), along with Toe Blake (centre) and Maurice "Rocket" Richard (left)

and his backhand shot was one of the best in the league. Béliveau was especially good at standing in front of the opposition net and keeping the puck away from defensemen who tried to check him. The Canadiens reclaimed the Stanley Cup in 1956, with Béliveau scoring 12 goals and 19 points in 10 playoff games as the Habs rolled over the New York Rangers and the Detroit Red Wings.

For the next five seasons, the Montreal Canadiens dominated the NHL. Not only did they win five straight championships, they finished in first place in the six-team league four times. They had the best goalie in Jacques Plante, the top defenceman in Doug Harvey and a high-powered attack led by Béliveau, Dickie Moore, Bernie Geoffrion, Bert Olmstead and the Richard brothers, Maurice and Henri. The forwards could score virtually at will and in one game against Boston, Béliveau set a record by scoring three goals in just 44 seconds! Each of those goals came on the power play, and the NHL eventually felt compelled to change the rules so that the player would be able to come out of the penalty box if a goal was scored before the full two minutes were up. It was one way they hoped to slow down Béliveau and the mighty Canadiens.

Béliveau was a consistent performer during the glory years of the Montreal dynasty. Despite some brief injury problems, he produced more than a point per game, and in 1958–59 he once again led the league in goals with 45. He never produced fewer than 74 points when he played a full season. Recognition came in many forms for Béliveau, including selection to the NHL's first All-Star Team in 1955, 1956, 1957 and 1959, and second team honours in 1958. He was named winner of the Hart Memorial Trophy as the Most Valuable Player in 1956 and took home the Art Ross Trophy for the most points that year.

"He's tremendously strong, a beautiful skater, already a superb stickhandler, strictly a team man with a perfect sense of playmaking," Detroit coach Tommy Ivan once said of Béliveau. "He has a wonderfully hard and accurate shot. He'd be a star on any hockey club. I wish he were on mine."

Béliveau was not only talented, he was very poised and possessed a quick, accurate shot that helped him score many goals. He was an elegant skater and his well mannered, quiet style made him popular across the entire NHL.

By the start of the 1960–61 season, the legendary Rocket had decided to retire and, although the team was still strong, the Chicago Black Hawks ended the Montreal dynasty, edging them out in six games in the first round of the playoffs. More changes were on way, and one of the biggest

> "I wasn't even assistant captain before that and other players had more seniority than I did. I couldn't believe it when Toe Blake came out of the room, came over to shake my hand and told everyone I was their new captain. It was an incredible honour. I wasn't expecting it."

was the naming of Jean Béliveau as team captain. Many, including Béliveau himself, had expected Geoffrion to be named the new leader of the Habs, but Béliveau was really the natural choice. His serious and thoughtful manner commanded respect both on and off the ice.

The Canadiens were now Béliveau's team, but it would be a long time before he would hoist the Stanley Cup as its captain.

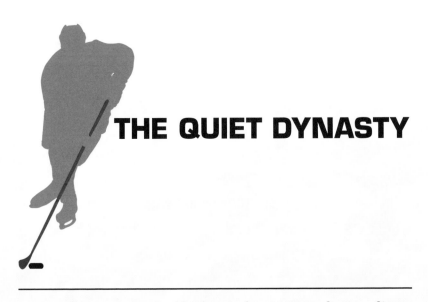

THE QUIET DYNASTY

Jean Béliveau once said about the Montreal Canadiens, "We think the Stanley Cup is the important thing. We feel we are representing French Canada and winning the Cup for our supporters is the main objective." That's what made the championship drought the Canadiens endured between 1961 and 1964 so difficult for Béliveau and his teammates. Montreal was by no means a bad team — they finished in first place three of those four seasons — but each year saw them eliminated in the first round of the playoffs. The team had lost many players with Béliveau, Henri Richard, Ralph Backstrom, Jean-Guy Talbot and Claude Provost being the only significant holdovers from the dynasty of the fifties.

For Béliveau the early sixties represented a time of great doubt and many significant injuries. Questions were raised about his heart. It had been said as early as 1953 that Béliveau's heart would not support his large body. A "cardiac anomaly" was the term given to his condition, and some speculated that he would not be able to withstand the stress of professional hockey. After a 32-goal, 90-point season in 1960–61, Béliveau slipped down to 18 goals in each of the next two seasons, although he was still at a point-per-game pace. The media attacked the Canadiens captain, and Béliveau thought about retirement. Montreal management would not hear of his intention to retire, however, and had him checked out thoroughly by doctors. It was determined that Béliveau's body had adjusted to his condition and that he was in no danger if he continued his playing career.

"Hockey is a game that demands physical strength and endurance and you can get hurt playing it. It's like life that way. But you don't have to be violent."

By the start of the 1963–64 season Béliveau was back to his old self, scoring 28 goals and adding 50 assists for 78 points. His performance earned him his second Hart Trophy, and the Habs were a contender once again. The team was remade by new general manager Sam Pollock with the addition of talented players like Yvan Cournoyer, Dick Duff, Gump Worsley and Rogie Vachon.

After Montreal took back the Stanley Cup in 1965, Béliveau led his revitalized team to the Cup again in 1966, 1968 and 1969. Four championships in five years, with a good but not powerful team, had many calling this era of Canadiens history "the quiet dynasty." Béliveau was at his best during the playoffs during this era, earning the Conn Smythe Trophy in 1965. In 1966 he had 10 points in 10 games as the Canadiens edged out Detroit for the Cup.

The Canadiens really wanted to win the Stanley Cup in 1967, Canada's centennial year. They wanted to display the trophy at Expo '67, which was to be held in Montreal that summer. Béliveau was strong in the playoffs, coming back after a very serious eye injury shortened his season to 11 points in 10 games. But the upstart Toronto Maple Leafs interrupted the Canadiens' attempt to win five consecutive titles once again by knocking off Montreal in six games in the Finals.

The 1967–68 season started off badly for Béliveau and the Canadiens: the team got off to a very slow start and their captain was hobbled by an injury. But Béliveau returned to the ice in December, earning his 1,000th career point and leading the Habs to the first post-expansion championship as they wiped out the first-year St. Louis Blues in four straight games. Béliveau injured his leg in the first game of the Finals against the Blues but came out on Montreal Forum ice on crutches to accept the Stanley Cup on behalf of his teammates.

The next season, unknown Claude Ruel took over as the Habs coach and he counted on Béliveau to help him adjust to his new role. Young players were put on Béliveau's line, and he told all of them to play their game and that

Béliveau comes around the net.

he would make the necessary adjustments — a gracious gesture considering his stature.

Even with a rookie coach, Montreal was better in 1968–69, and Béliveau had one of his best seasons with 33 goals and 82 points. He was just as good in the playoffs, with 5 goals, and led all scorers with 10 assists. The Canadiens faced the tough Boston Bruins, led by Bobby Orr, in the semifinals. The teams split the first four games of the series, but Montreal won the fifth. The sixth game at the Boston Garden went into overtime. In the second overtime period, Provost dug out a puck along the boards to Béliveau who quickly snapped a shot over the shoulder of Boston netminder Gerry Cheevers. It was Béliveau's first and only overtime winning goal in the playoffs, and he smiled broadly. Montreal once again cruised to a four game sweep of the St. Louis Blues in the Finals, and the season ended with the Montreal captain leaving the ice with the Stanley Cup once again — an image that had become familiar to so many Canadians.

ONE MORE YEAR

The 1969–70 season was a year the Montreal Canadiens would like to forget. As defending Stanley Cup champions, the Habs were once again favoured to be a contender in the NHL's East Division, but they didn't even make the playoffs! Béliveau himself did not have a stellar season, with just 19 goals and 49 points in 63 games played. Once again he felt it was time to retire, but Montreal general manager Sam Pollock asked him to play one more year so that younger players could continue to learn from him. Béliveau agreed to the request, but made it clear the 1970–71 campaign would be his last.

The Canadiens did not have an especially strong season, finishing in third place in the East, but Béliveau played in 70 games, scoring 25 times and adding 51 assists to help get his team back into the playoffs. Béliveau's most memorable night of the season came on February 11,

1971, when the Canadiens hosted the Minnesota North Stars. The Montreal captain scored the 500th goal of his career during a 6–2 victory. For the milestone goal, his third of the night, Béliveau took passes from Phil Roberto and Frank Mahovlich before beating North Star netminder Gilles Gilbert to become just the fourth NHL player to reach the 500-goal mark.

In spite of Béliveau's strong performance during the regular season, few hockey experts predicted that the Canadiens would

> "Jean Béliveau is the best thing that has happened to modern hockey."
> —Conn Smythe

do much during the playoffs. The team made a coaching change during the season, which is rarely a good sign. But they made a couple of key player additions as well, securing high-scoring winger Frank Mahovlich in a major trade with Detroit, and making unknown Ken Dryden their starting goalie for the postseason. Montreal opened the playoffs against the heavily favoured Boston Bruins, but backed by Dryden's stellar netminding, the Canadiens pulled off a stunning upset in seven games.

Montreal beat Minnesota in the next round before facing Chicago for the Stanley Cup. The Black Hawks were on the verge of beating the Canadiens but could never nail down a key goal to kill the Montreal spirit. The Habs were even down 2–0 in the seventh and final game but rallied to score three straight times and hang on to a 3–2 win. Béliveau finished the playoffs with a record 16 assists and was presented with the Stanley Cup for the tenth and final time of his playing career.

Less then a month later, Béliveau announced that he was officially retiring.

"I've always believed that a public person should retire early rather than too late," he said. "I understand that some are not in a position to do this, but 1971 provided me with a perfect time to retire. I had an excellent season, was the top scorer on the team, and we won the Stanley Cup for my tenth time."

He left the league with 507 goals and 1,219 points in 1,125 regular season games, and as the NHL's all-time top playoff point producer, with 176 points in 162 post-season games. It was the end of a truly remarkable career which was perhaps best summarized by Prime Minister Pierre Elliot Trudeau, who said, "Rarely has the career of an athlete been so exemplary by his courage, his sense of discipline and honour, his lively intelligence and finesse and his magnificent team spirit. Béliveau has given new prestige to hockey."

Gordie Howe presents Béliveau with the Hart Memorial Trophy.

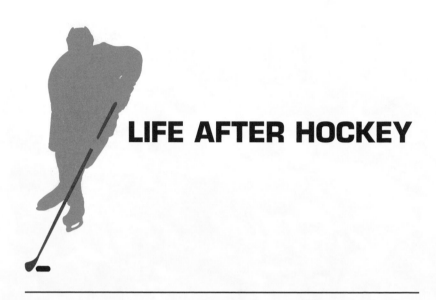

LIFE AFTER HOCKEY

After Jean Béliveau announced his retirement on June 9, 1971, he stepped into a new role as a vice-president of corporate relations for the Montreal Canadiens. It was an easy transition for Béliveau, who had worked for years with Molson Breweries, the owners of the Canadiens, in the off-season. Gracious and friendly with the public, Béliveau was the ideal candidate to represent the team at various functions and provide strong advice to coaches and managers of the team. He also helped out players whenever possible, including a new Montreal superstar named Guy Lafleur. The speedy right winger was drafted by Montreal just one day after Béliveau announced his retirement, and Lafleur stayed with Béliveau for a while as he got accustomed to Montreal and playing for the legendary team. Béliveau advised Lafleur, who grew up idolizing Béliveau and wore number 4 in junior just like his idol, to take a new sweater number and make every boy in Quebec want to wear it. Lafleur took the lesson to heart, and soon number 10 was the most revered Canadiens sweater among Montreal fans.

With his success on and off the ice, it was only natural that Jean Béliveau would be offered many opportunities after his retirement. One of the first was to return to the Coliseum to play for the Quebec Nordiques of the newly formed World Hockey Association, a rival league to the NHL that would start play in 1972. The Nordiques offered Béliveau $1 million, more than he had made in 18 NHL seasons combined, to join their organization, first as a player and then as an executive. It was more money than he had ever dreamed of, but in typical fashion Béliveau turned down the offer, saying that he could never play to the level they offered to pay.

Over the years Béliveau was often asked to run for political office and to take a seat in the Canadian Senate, but he declined the offers. Béliveau even turned down the opportunity to become the Governor General of Canada, as he felt that he needed to spend time with his granddaughters. Mylene and Magalie were the children of Béliveau's daughter Hélène. When her husband died suddenly, Jean and his wife Elise felt they had to do whatever they could for the family. Béliveau had been

"Gentleman Jean" with his number 4 replica jersey in the Hockey Hall of Fame in Toronto

taken aback when his former teammate Maurice Richard had put his own memorabilia up for auction, but now the idea appealed to the Béliveau family as well. Béliveau shocked the hockey world by putting much of his hockey memorabilia, such as rings, sweaters and sticks, up for sale. This ensured that his granddaughters could take in the proceeds while Béliveau was still able to help them manage the entire process. The auction proved to be very successful, and around a million dollars was spent by fans of the Canadiens legend.

Never out of the spotlight, Béliveau was not afraid to speak out during the NHL lockout in 2004. He told NHL players that the fight they were engaged in with management was not one they were going to win. As a former executive with an NHL team, Béliveau knew how many teams were losing money and that many jobs were at stake. He also spoke out about how the game of hockey was slowing down with all the hooking, holding and interference. Béliveau once stated, "Fast skating, sharp passing, smart clean defensive play, that's hockey." Although he was not part of the formal process of review, his comments were taken very seriously and played a part in changing the game for the better.

Although his career ended in 1971, Béliveau remains a hero to many. In 2009, while he was aboard the International Space Station, Canadian astronaut Bob

Thirsk asked to chat with the legendary hockey star through a video link. Thirsk had brought along a photo of Béliveau in his Montreal uniform for his visit in space. But one of the most unusual tributes came from brothers Chip and Tom Hunter of Florenceville, New Brunswick, who designed a 600-foot (183-metre) long corn maze in the likeness of Béliveau, in a six-acre (two-and-a-half hectare) field. The design is based on a famous photo of Béliveau striding up the ice carrying the puck, with his head up. The brothers expected over 7,000 visitors to walk through their Béliveau maze!

Jean Béliveau stayed in his official front office role with the Canadiens until August 31, 1993, his sixty-second birthday. During his time there, the Habs won another seven Stanley Cups (1973, 1976, 1977, 1978, 1979, 1986 and 1993) to put the Béliveau name on the silver trophy a total of 17 times — a total nobody else can boast. To this day his stature among hockey fans still remains as high as ever. One of the reasons is that Béliveau always understood the impact of television and understood that he could be a role model for many. He once said, "I have to set an example. It's amazing what the kids will pick up from you. They want to do things just the way you do them."

Béliveau certainly made a special impression on a young man named Wayne Gretzky. "The Great One" watched Béliveau on *Hockey Night in Canada* when he was a little boy, and his father Walter told Wayne that Béliveau was thoughtful, intelligent and humble. Gretzky noticed how gracious Béliveau was when his team won, and also how often the Montreal captain was on the winning side.

Respected by everyone, Jean Béliveau will always be considered a hockey icon. Béliveau has said that he considers himself to be a proud Canadian and Canadien. No hockey fan would have it any other way.

> "Jean Béliveau was the first guy that was able to play the game elegantly, without having to be rough, without having to fight... In a lot of ways my play was more like his than anyone."
>
> —Wayne Gretzky

JEAN BÉLIVEAU

Born: August 31, 1931, in Trois-
Rivières, Quebec

Height: 6 ft 3 in (1.91 m)

Weight: 205 lb (93 kg)

Position: Centre

Shot: Left

Pro clubs: Montreal Canadiens

Playing career: 1950–1971

Hall of Fame: 1972

REGULAR SEASON

Season	Team	GP	G	A	PTS	PIM
1950–51	Montreal Canadiens	2	1	1	2	0
1952–53	Montreal Canadiens	3	5	0	5	0
1953–54	Montreal Canadiens	44	13	21	34	22
1954–55	Montreal Canadiens	70	37	36	73	58
1955–56	Montreal Canadiens	70	47	41	88	143
1956–57	Montreal Canadiens	69	33	51	84	105
1957–58	Montreal Canadiens	55	27	32	59	93
1958–59	Montreal Canadiens	64	45	46	91	67
1959–60	Montreal Canadiens	60	34	40	74	57
1960–61	Montreal Canadiens	69	32	58	90	57
1961–62	Montreal Canadiens	43	18	23	41	36
1962–63	Montreal Canadiens	69	18	49	67	68
1963–64	Montreal Canadiens	68	28	50	78	42
1964–65	Montreal Canadiens	58	20	23	43	76
1965–66	Montreal Canadiens	67	29	48	77	50
1966–67	Montreal Canadiens	53	12	26	38	22
1967–68	Montreal Canadiens	59	31	37	68	28
1968–69	Montreal Canadiens	69	33	49	82	55
1969–70	Montreal Canadiens	63	19	30	49	10
1970–71	Montreal Canadiens	70	25	51	76	40
NHL Totals		**1125**	**507**	**712**	**1219**	**1029**

PLAYOFFS

Season	Team	GP	G	A	PTS	PIM
1953–1954	Montreal Canadiens	10	2	8	10	4
1954–1955	Montreal Canadiens	12	6	7	13	18
1955–1956	Montreal Canadiens	10	12	7	19	22
1956–1957	Montreal Canadiens	10	6	6	12	15
1957–1958	Montreal Canadiens	10	4	8	12	10
1958–1959	Montreal Canadiens	3	1	4	5	4
1959–1960	Montreal Canadiens	8	5	2	7	6
1960–1961	Montreal Canadiens	6	0	5	5	0
1961–1962	Montreal Canadiens	6	2	1	3	4
1962–1963	Montreal Canadiens	5	2	1	3	2
1963–1964	Montreal Canadiens	5	2	0	2	18
1964–1965	Montreal Canadiens	13	8	8	16	34
1965–1966	Montreal Canadiens	10	5	5	10	6
1966–1967	Montreal Canadiens	10	6	5	11	26
1967–1968	Montreal Canadiens	10	7	4	11	6
1968–1969	Montreal Canadiens	14	5	10	15	8
1970–1971	Montreal Canadiens	20	6	16	22	28
NHL Totals		**162**	**79**	**97**	**176**	**211**

WAYNE
GRETZKY

CAN HE WIN A STANLEY CUP?

The Edmonton Oilers were set to play their 99th game of the season as they took to the ice on the night of May 19, 1984. The hometown Oilers were greeted with wild cheers from an adoring crowd which hoped that Edmonton was about to put an end to the dynasty of the New York Islanders — winners of the Cup for the past four seasons. The young Oilers were just one win away from wresting the championship from the Islanders, holding a 3–1 lead in games. But the pressure was on Edmonton, who needed to win on home ice or head back to play the final two games back in front of a hostile New York crowd. Although the Oilers had been a Cup contender for the last three years, they'd never won a championship. And just a year before, they'd lost in the Finals to the Islanders who swept them in four straight games.

The spotlight would, of course, be on Wayne Gretzky.

The superbly talented Edmonton centre had been held scoreless against New York in the 1983 Finals, and had only recently started to produce in this year's series. Two goals in the fourth game helped carry the Oilers to a resounding 7–2 win, but now the Cup was on the line. Could The Great One do it? As team captain, could Gretzky help his team triumph over the Islanders?

Gretzky was indeed The Great One. It seemed as though he'd been waiting for this moment his whole hockey career. He scored two first period goals, one on a breakaway and another when he ripped home a pass from teammate Jari Kurri. The Oilers added two more in the second for a 4–0 lead going into the third. But then the Islanders put a little scare into the crowd with a pair of goals early in the third. Good goaltending from Andy Moog helped the Oilers as the New York club pressed to keep their crown. Soon the clock was winding down and, with the Edmonton crowd in a frenzy, the Oilers added an empty-net goal to make it 5–2. The Oilers jumped for joy and, as the clock ticked off the final seconds, *Hockey Night in Canada* announcer Bob Cole exclaimed, "The Oilers have won the Stanley Cup!"

The relieved Edmonton club mobbed their goalie as they celebrated their first ever Stanley Cup. NHL president John Zeigler brought out the coveted trophy and then Gretzky raised it over his head. It was a victory not only for the team, but for its young captain.

As he was interviewed by reporters, Gretzky was almost at a loss for words. "I don't know how to describe it," he said emotionally. "We played tremendous hockey. We played well the whole series. I've waited 25 years for this. They were great champions. We hope we can be as good as they are."

When interviewed for the *Toronto Star*, Gretzky said, "When the NHL president gave me the Cup on the ice, my mind flashed to a picture I'd seen of Jean Béliveau receiving the Cup one time when Montreal won it. Now it's me. A dream come true."

The Oilers would prove to be champions themselves, and they went on to create their own dynasty behind the leadership and great play of Wayne Gretzky. He would have many more great nights in the NHL, but few would ever match the night he won his first Stanley Cup.

THE KID FROM BRANTFORD

Wayne Gretzky's father, Walter, grew up on a farm on the Nith River, near Canning, Ontario. He played Junior B hockey and was a smart player with good finesse skills, but, although he got a tryout with the Toronto Marlboroughs, he was told that he wasn't good enough to make it at the highest junior level. When his hockey career was over, he began working for Bell Canada, where he remained for the next 34 years.

When he was 19, Walter met a girl named Phyliss Hockin, who also liked to play sports. They were married in 1960 and moved to the nearby city of Brantford, where they raised a family of five: Wayne, born January 26, 1961, and then Kim, Keith, Glen and Brent. The family emphasized sports for all of them, believing participation would help keep them happy and out of trouble, although they never pushed any of them to do something they did not like.

When Wayne turned two, Walter got him out on

Gretzky, around age 7, on the ice at his home in Brantford

skates at a local park. He could barely contain his son's enthusiasm. Wayne was so insistent on learning to skate and play hockey that Walter decided he'd better build a rink in the backyard if he wanted to stay warm. So Walter built "Wally's Coliseum," as it became known, in the backyard of 42 Varadi Avenue. Now Wayne could play before school, after classes and all day on the weekends, while his father could stay warm in the house. A clothesline with lights served as backyard lighting, allowing Wayne to practise long into the night. His father helped him develop his skills by giving him drills and exercises. For example, Walter would use empty detergent bottles as pylons for Wayne to stickhandle around, and he used a picnic table to block a good portion of the net so that Wayne could practice hitting the corners of the goal.

As so many Canadians have, Wayne grew up watching *Hockey Night in Canada*, usually at his grandmother Mary's farm. She loved Frank Mahovlich of the Toronto Maple Leafs, while Wayne cheered on superstar Gordie Howe of the Detroit Red Wings.

Wayne even worked on his skills while watching televised games. He would draw a rink on a piece of paper, then trace the path of the puck without taking his pen off the paper. This showed him where the puck spent most of the time, and helped him develop the uncanny ability to follow his father's top rule: "Don't go where the puck is; go where the puck is going to be." These words would become famous.

On those nights at the farm, his grandmother was also very willing to act as Wayne's goalie when he tried to score on her with a small souvenir stick and a plastic puck. And it was she who took Wayne to his first NHL game at Maple Leaf Gardens to see the Leafs play the Oakland Seals.

By the time he was six, Wayne desperately wanted to play on a team. But there was no organized hockey for kids below the age of ten in Brantford. Walter managed to arrange a tryout and, because of his superior skating, Wayne was selected for the Brantford Nadrofsky Steelers — a team of ten-year-olds. He didn't get that much ice time, but he did score one goal during the 1967–68 season. It was a start. He produced even more the next season, scoring 27 times. During his third year with the Steelers — still just eight years old — he scored 104 times in 62 games. In the 1970–71 season he tallied 196 goals in 76 games. Now everyone was talking about the gifted young boy from Brantford. But this would soon pose a problem.

LEAVING HOME FOR TORONTO

When the 1971–72 season began, Gretzky was 10 years old and scoring goals at an astounding rate. *Toronto Telegram* hockey writer John Iaboni visited Brantford in October of 1971 to look at the player people were now calling "The Great Gretzky." Iaboni noted that Gretzky had scored five times and added two assists in a recent game, and that he was wearing sweater number nine in honour of Gordie Howe. Iaboni was also impressed that he played centre, played defense, killed penalties and was a power-play specialist. Gretzky, the story stated, led his team to championships.

Knowing that Wayne was an exceptional hockey player, Walter Gretzky told his son that he'd be watched all the time, and that it was important for him to play his best every time out. It was a lesson well learned even at the tender age of ten: that season Wayne scored 378 times in 85 games for the Steelers.

But Gretzky was a quiet and reserved boy, and the attention he started to receive bothered him. The attention wasn't coming from teammates or other players, but rather from parents and some coaches. Gretzky was taunted, ridiculed and even threatened. Many accused him of being a "puck hog," even though he had plenty of assists. If the team lost, it would be put on Wayne's shoulders, and if he was checked, the crowd would cheer. All of this was starting to take the joy out of playing the game he loved.

Luckily Gretzky loved the game more than he hated what was being said about him, and he was always ready to

"Now, Gordie Howe is my kind of player. He had so many tricks around the net no wonder he scored so many goals. I'd like to be just like him."

play his best the next time. Bob Hockin, his coach (who was also his uncle) recalled a tournament game with his team down 5–0. Gretzky came to the bench for a brief rest. Hockin told his star player (who had played nearly the entire 60 minutes) that he could win the game on his own. Gretzky went out and scored six straight goals to give his team the win.

And Gretzky just kept getting better. The following season, he scored 50 goals in a nine-game tournament in Hespeler, Ontario. Then, on April 10, 1974, Gretzky scored the 1,000th goal of his minor hockey career.

Gretzky, age 11, with his idol, Gordie Howe

But not everyone felt that Gretzky was a superstar player. In the 1974 Quebec International Pee Wee tournament, Gretzky's team lost. The coach of the Oshawa team, who was a former NHL defenseman, said he would rather have his star player than Gretzky.

One day in February 1975, Wayne was playing at Maple Leaf Gardens on "Brantford Day." As he was introduced, he was booed by parents. The 14-year-old was driven to tears. He was inconsolable and nobody could explain to him why this was happening. The incident may have been what finally drove him out of his hometown forever. He pleaded with his father to let him go to Toronto where he would not be in the headlines every day. Concerned that his son would fall prey to the dangers of life in a large city like Toronto, Walter steadfastly refused at first. Wayne pointed out to his father that he could get into trouble right in Brantford if he chose, and soon Walter, knowing full well Wayne's future was going to be in hockey, was on the phone with his contacts to get his son placed in the Toronto area.

Once word got out that Gretzky wanted to move to Toronto, there were those who did everything they could to keep him out. In order to make the move, Gretzky had to play above his age group once again. For the next two years Gretzky played Junior B hockey in Vaughan, Ontario, which meant that as a 14-year-old, he was playing against men as old as 20. There was great concern that Wayne would get hurt playing against older players, but when he scored two goals in his first game with the Nationals, everyone — including his father — was convinced there was no need to worry. It took a while for Gretzky to adjust, but he scored 27 times (in just 28 games) his first season playing for the Vaughan Nationals and 36 times in only 32 games playing for the renamed Seneca Nationals in 1976–77.

Gretzky certainly missed his family during the hockey season, and at times it was a very lonely existence, but at least he had some privacy. And, as he started his junior career, he would be faced with a new challenge.

BREAKAWAY TO THE WORLD HOCKEY ASSOCIATION

In 1977, the Sault Ste. Marie Greyhounds of the Ontario Hockey Association (OHA) drafted Wayne Gretzky third overall. But he had no intention of ever playing for them. Sixteen-year-old Gretzky didn't want to be so far away from home. But Greyhounds manager Angelo Bumbacco convinced the Gretzky family to come visit the Soo. Once they arrived, the Gretzkys met up with Steve Bodnar, a minor hockey teammate from Wayne's days in Brantford, and his family. It was agreed that if Gretzky played for the Greyhounds, he would stay with the Bodnar family. Wayne felt so comfortable with that idea that he quickly changed his mind and agreed to play in the Soo for the 1977–78 season. He was also assured that his education would be paid for, in case he was injured and unable to play hockey anymore.

Muzz MacPherson, coach of the Greyhounds, let Gretzky

Gretzky during the 1978 Ontario Major Junior Hockey League (now Ontario Hockey League) All-Star game in Windsor, Ontario

play the game he played best. It was here that he started working his magic from behind the net, something he would become known for in the NHL. Taking the puck behind the goal allowed Gretzky to see everything in front of him and make the plays he needed to make. His assist total quickly started to rise. And, although he'd started off his hockey career with number 9, he started wearing number 99. He'd actually wanted number 9, but another player on the team had that number. After he tried sweater numbers 19 and 14, the coach suggested he try 99. The first night he wore the new number, Gretzky scored three times. The number 99 would go down as the most famous number in hockey history.

That season, Gretzky was named OHA Rookie of the Year, scoring 70 goals and 112 assists for 182 points in just 64 games. He added 26 points in 13 playoff games, and also played for Team Canada at the World Junior tournament. Although Canada didn't win the gold medal, Wayne tallied 17 points (8 goals and 9 assists) in 9 games.

It was a very successful year for Wayne personally, but the next year the Greyhounds made a change in coaches and Gretzky didn't agree with the strategies of Paul Theriault. The new bench boss wanted to change Gretzky's style, despite his great success, and it soon became clear that Wayne would not return to the Soo for another year.

By this time, he had one of the best agents in the business, Gus Badali. Badali started to look at alternatives for Gretzky, and even though he was only 17, the World Hockey Association (WHA) was willing to sign him. The WHA was a professional hockey league that wanted to rival the NHL. Although the league had been around since 1972, it was still struggling to sell tickets. It hoped that Gretzky would attract more fans. Nelson Skalbania, owner of the Indianapolis Racers, signed Gretzky to a personal services deal, paying him $250,000 just to sign. (This meant that the contract was with Skalbania, not the team, which meant Skalbania could pay it or sell it off.) Gretzky also earned a salary of $100,000 in the first year, $150,000 in the second year and $175,000 by the fourth year of the contract. Just the previous summer Gretzky had been making five dollars an hour filling potholes while working for a road crew. It was quite the pay increase.

Gretzky's career as a Racer lasted all of eight games (he scored three goals and added three assists) before Skalbania told him he couldn't afford his contract because no one was coming out to games. Offered a choice of where he was to be traded, Gretzky chose Edmonton, which had a new arena, over Winnipeg, and soon found himself on a plane to Alberta.

"Nelson Skalbania called me and said, 'I'm losing too much money; I gotta trade you. Do you want to go to Winnipeg or Edmonton?' I wanted to go to Edmonton because they had a better chance of getting into the NHL," Gretzky said, reflecting on the trade.

Peter Pocklington, owner of the Edmonton Oilers, paid Skalbania $850,000 for Gretzky and two other players. Gretzky finished the 1978–79 season with the team, playing in 72 games and recording 43 goals and 103 points. The Oilers lost the WHA final to Winnipeg, but that was okay: Gretzky had realized a childhood dream, playing alongside his idol, Gordie Howe (who had come out of retirement to join the new league) during the WHA All-Star game. Howe, the NHL's all-time leader in goals and points, predicted that one day Gretzky would break all his records.

When Gretzky turned 18 on January 26, 1979, he signed a deal with the Oilers that would keep him in Edmonton until 1999. Pocklington was anxious to get Gretzky signed to a long-term deal to keep him away from the NHL. The WHA was looking to merge with the NHL for the next season, and Pocklington wanted Gretzky to lead the team. The merger took place in the middle of the season, and the Oilers were allowed to keep Gretzky even though all other players his age in the WHA had to go through the NHL Entry Draft. However, the NHL ruled that Gretzky would not be allowed to compete for the Rookie of the Year award, since he had played professional hockey for one season with the WHA (Gretzky had been named the top first-year player in the WHA).

As well as Gretzky had performed throughout his hockey

career, there were those who doubted that he could do it in the NHL. He was considered too small and too slow, and some pointed out that he certainly wasn't tough. None of this affected Gretzky at all. He wasn't overwhelmed by the type of play in the NHL, and firmly believed he could be a great player. He proved all the critics wrong by scoring 51 goals while leading the league in assists with 96. His point total of 137 tied him with Marcel Dionne of the Los Angeles Kings for the best in the league, but Dionne was given the Art Ross Trophy because he had scored one more goal. Still, Gretzky was awarded the Hart Memorial Trophy as the Most Valuable Player in the league.

Gretzky had erased any doubt that he could survive in the NHL, and as the Oilers started to draft other star players, the Edmonton club would soon dominate the NHL for the better part of the next ten years.

A GREAT HOCKEY
TEAM

When Gretzky first arrived in Edmonton, Oilers coach and general manager Glen Sather told him that the team would not only join the NHL, but that he would one day captain the team.

Even veteran Oilers' goalie Ron Low made a bold prediction: "This team will be playing in the Stanley Cup Finals in three years. Any team with Wayne Gretzky on it has to be. He's that good."

But as talented as Gretzky was, there was no way he could win the Stanley Cup on his own. So Sather and his staff assembled a great team around him. Future Hall of Fame players Mark Messier, Paul Coffey, Grant Fuhr, Jari Kurri and Glenn Anderson all began careers with Edmonton. With this great team, the Oilers first made a significant mark in the 1981 playoffs when they upset the mighty Montreal Canadiens (led by superstar Guy Lafleur)

Gretzky celebrates his first Stanley Cup victory.

in three straight games in the first round of the playoffs. However, the next season they lost to the rather lowly Los Angeles Kings in the first round. Many began to question if the Oilers had the right stuff to win when it mattered most. Rather than make a lot of changes, Sather was smart enough to know that it was just a question of time before his superstar team would win it all. His team was built perfectly for the game in the 1980s — a high energy, offensively oriented club that could fly up and down the ice easily.

As the Oilers learned to win, Gretzky was tearing apart the NHL

> "I've got to score. That's just the way it is."

record book. In 1981–82 he scored a record 92 goals and totalled 212 points. He also reached the 50-goal mark in one season — in only his 39th game of the year. This shattered the record held by Maurice Richard and Mike Bossy, who had scored 50 times in their first 50 games of the season. In typical Gretzky style, he scored five goals in the game played on December 30, 1981, to hit the 50 mark. Gretzky would record over 200 points in a season twice more with the Oilers, and notch 100 or more assists in eight consecutive years with Edmonton. He never scored fewer than 51 goals as an Oiler, and he took home the Art Ross Trophy eight straight times. He also won the Hart Memorial Trophy eight times while in Edmonton.

Such a remarkable performance brought Gretzky worldwide fame and endorsement opportunities he had never before imagined. Gretzky was a spokesperson for insurance, clothing, breakfast cereal, chocolate bar, soft drink, lunch box and table hockey companies, to name just a few. Walter helped guide his son through all the offers to use Wayne's likeness and image. Wayne was also named *Sports Illustrated*'s Sportsman of the Year in 1982, a rare feat for a hockey player (Bobby Orr was the only other one) and even rarer for a Canadian-born athlete.

Gretzky played hockey like nobody else had ever had. He had grown to 5'11" (1.8 metres) and weighed about 180 pounds (82 kilograms) and realized he couldn't play a physical game and survive. So he took refuge behind the net to help set up many goals.

"Other teams didn't know how to defend against me when I set up behind the net," he said about his favourite position, a place that became known as 'Gretzky's office.' "My teammates became more at ease with it. As they became more comfortable, that made it difficult for the opposing team to cover them. . . . We made it hard for teams to defend. They didn't know exactly what to do."

"He's worse than Bobby Orr," said Philadelphia Flyers' player Bobby Clarke. "At least Orr started in his own end and you could brace yourself. Gretzky just materializes out of nowhere."

Gretzky with the 1996 Jean Béliveau Trophy, given by Hockey Canada

He also learned to use the boards by banking the puck off the wooden frame and then chasing it down. Gretzky would drive defenceman crazy by taking the puck down the ice and then circling at the blueline when everyone thought he was going straight to the net. By curling as he entered the attacking zone, he had a great chance to spot an open man for a clear shot. He often worked this play to perfection with winger Jari Kurri. Not the fastest player in the league, Gretzky could somehow find another gear when he had to, and, although his shot was not the hardest, it was the most accurate. One of his most memorable goals came in overtime against the Calgary Flames in the 1988 playoffs when he drilled a shot over the arm of netminder Mike Vernon from outside the faceoff circle. Vernon barely moved and the Flames were quickly eliminated in four games.

So Ron Low's prediction was pretty accurate: the Oilers made it to the Stanley Cup Finals in 1983, losing to the Islanders in four straight games. Sather had built up the team with great goaltending and defence with players like Andy Moog, Lee Fogolin and Kevin Lowe. Other talented forwards included Mike Krushelnyski, Dave Semenko and Keith Acton.

But once the Oilers won their first Cup, they gained the confidence they needed to win multiple championships. They took the Cup in 1984, 1985, 1987 and 1988. Only a lucky goal by the Flames in 1986 stopped the Oilers from a shot at five straight titles. Many compared this group of Oilers to the great Montreal Canadiens teams of the 1950s and 1970s. As the Oilers gathered for a team photo after their 1988 win on home ice after beating Boston, some wondered how many Cups this team could win since many players were in their prime years. At the age of 27, Gretzky could still look forward to at least four more great years as an Oiler before he would become a free agent.

However, in the dressing room after the final game against the Bruins, Walter Gretzky greeted Wayne with some shocking news.

Gretzky plays against his old team.

THE TRADE THAT SHOCKED A NATION

Peter Pocklington wanted to sign Wayne Gretzky to a new contract even though he had signed a new deal worth $1.5 million a year ín 1987 (his old 21-year deal had since been torn up). The problem was that this would take Gretzky to the age of 31. After that he would become an unrestricted free agent, which meant that he could walk away from the Oilers and they would get nothing for the best player in the game. Pocklington toyed with the idea of putting shares of the Oilers up for sale, but in order to do that, he needed Gretzky, his biggest asset, signed to a longer-term deal. There were stories circulating that Pocklington needed cash to help his other businesses. The Edmonton owner also came to see Gretzky as a diminishing asset since Wayne was getting older despite his record-setting performances in the playoffs (he led the NHL in playoff scoring four times as an Oiler). Of course, other NHL clubs were quite willing to pay a high price for Gretzky's services. The Los Angeles Kings were hot on the Gretzky trail and convinced Pocklington to at least consider the idea of trading him to them.

Meanwhile, Gretzky married actress Janet Jones in Edmonton on July 16, 1988, in what many called "Canada's Royal Wedding." It was Gretzky's last moment of bliss in Edmonton: he soon received a surprising phone call from Kings owner Bruce McNall, who told him he had permission from Pocklington to approach him about a trade. An irate Gretzky called his father and told him that he was through as an Oiler. Word quickly leaked out, and by August 9, the Oilers had no choice but to confirm the deal. As much as Gretzky wanted to stay in Edmonton and continue playing on a great team, he saw a good opportunity to become the highest paid player in the NHL, a distinction he richly deserved, and perhaps an opportunity for his wife to resume her acting career in Los Angeles. Gretzky could also see that Edmonton would not be able to support the Oilers to the point where they could keep all their top players.

It was a tearful goodbye for Gretzky, but his mind was made up.

> "I knew this thing would be big. But I had no idea it would be this big."

"I truly respect all the fans over the years," he said at a press conference as he squeezed a tissue. He dabbed at his eyes, trying to fight back the tears. Finally, he stepped away from the table and tried to compose himself. Across Canada, many felt that a national treasure had been sold to the Americans.

The Kings were not a great team and had given up Jimmy Carson, a 50-goal scorer, as well as some high draft choices and $15 million to Edmonton to land Gretzky. Showing a talent for good managerial skills himself, Gretzky helped McNall take a couple of Oilers players (Marty McSorley and Mike Krushelnyski) with him to Los Angeles.

In his first year as a King, Gretzky won the Hart Memorial Trophy one more time with a 168-point performance and took his team past the Oilers in a seven game series in the playoffs. It was with Los Angeles that Gretzky became the NHL's all-time leader in points besting Gordie Howe's mark of 1,850 right in Edmonton and then scoring his 802nd career goal to beat Howe's long-held mark of 801 NHL goals.

"I broke Gordie Howe's all-time record for assists. The old record was 1,049. That's an achievement I'm really proud of," said Gretzky. "I broke that record in 681 games. . . . You'll never catch me bragging about goals, but I'll talk all you want about my assists. Hockey is a team game, and to me, assists are the ultimate 'team' stat."

Although Gretzky piled up his own individual records, his team still struggled. But in 1992–93, the Kings made it to the Finals for the first time in team history. Wayne missed most of the first part of the regular season, but he was in top form in the playoffs. He gave what many believe to be his greatest performance in the seventh game of the Western Conference Finals when the Kings beat Toronto 5–4 at Maple Leaf Gardens.

"In my estimation this was the best game I ever played in the NHL," he said that night, "because it was game seven, it was on the road and it felt like the LA Kings versus Canada, not just the Maple Leafs. I don't think anyone expected us to win, but we did, 5–4. I had three goals and an assist."

Gretzky always played superbly in Toronto and he scored three times in the game to take his team past the Maple Leafs. It was his last truly great moment in the NHL and as always he made it memorable.

THE FINAL YEARS

By the 1995–96 season, the Kings were just an average team in the NHL. Gretzky looked for a change. That season he was traded to the St. Louis Blues, but only for the last part of the season and the playoffs.

As a free agent for the first time in his career, Gretzky sought to play for the Toronto Maple Leafs, a team he grew up watching. The Leafs' ownership failed to sign the national icon and it looked as though he would head to Vancouver. However, when the Canucks insisted he sign right away, Gretzky walked away to the New York Rangers where he played the final three years of his illustrious career. He twice led the league in assists while he played in the Big Apple.

Gretzky had always found time to play for Canada every time he was asked, no matter how tired or worn down he might have felt. He knew it was expected of him, and he never considered turning down the requests. During the 1987 Canada Cup tournament, he had provided hockey fans with a great thrill when he teamed with Mario Lemieux of the Pittsburgh Penguins, setting up Lemieux for the winning goal against Canada's archrivals, the Soviets. The last time he put on the Team Canada uniform was for the 1998 Winter Olympic Games in Nagano, Japan. He didn't score, but had four assists in six games. He was inexplicably kept on the bench during the shootout and when Canada was eliminated.

Gretzky's final season was not an especially good one — the Rangers missed the playoffs. In 70 games in 1998–99, he scored just nine times — by far his lowest total in the NHL. Late in the season, speculation began that Gretzky would retire. He made it official when he announced on April 16 that his next game would be his last in the NHL. The Pittsburgh Penguins won the final game of Gretzky's career with a 2–1 victory in overtime on April 18, 1999 in New York, but not before he had one last assist, the 1,963rd of his NHL career on a goal scored by Brian Leetch. Gretzky skated around the ice at Madison Square Garden and waved to the star-studded New York crowd before leaving the ice for the final time.

"When it was all over I didn't want to take my uniform off," he said of his last game. "I kept it on for about an hour and a half, the longest I had ever worn it after a game. I

Gretzky hangs up his final skate at his last NHL game.

knew that when I took it off, it would be for the last time, so I just took my time. But when I finally did hang up my skates and take off my sweater that final time, only one thing went through my mind: 'I'm sorry it's over but I know I made the right decision.'" It was difficult for Gretzky to stay out of hockey despite the demands of raising a large family. He and

> "I will never play again. The next time you see me skating will be with my kids."

his wife have five children: Paulina, Ty, Trevor, Tristan and Emma Marie. In May 2000, he was offered a part ownership of the Phoenix Coyotes. He eventually coached the team from 2005 to 2009, although he did not have great success behind the bench. When the team was placed into bankruptcy in 2009, Gretzky felt it best that he resign. Being out of hockey for the first time since he was a young boy allowed him some other pleasures, like watching his oldest son play football. Still, it seems likely that he will end up back in hockey at some point because he loves the game so much.

Before Gretzky played his final game, the NHL had announced that they were retiring his number league-wide. It was an appropriate tribute to a player who finished his NHL career with 894 goals and 2,857 points (both all-time NHL records) in 1,487 games played over 20 seasons.

Reflecting on his life in hockey, Gretzky said, "My career

in the NHL has given me a wonderful life, full of family, good friends and memories."

The statistics, the incredible number of awards, his passion for the game, the four Stanley Cup wins and his 61 career records he held at retirement show that Wayne Gretzky truly was "The Great One."

WAYNE GRETZKY

Born: January 26, 1961, in
  Brantford, Ontario

Height: 6 ft 0 in (1.82 m)

Weight: 185 lb (84 kg)

Position: Centre

Shot: Left

Pro clubs: Edmonton Oilers, Los
  Angeles Kings, St. Louis
  Blues, New York Rangers

Playing career: 1978–1999

Hall of Fame: 1999

REGULAR SEASON

Season	Team	GP	G	A	PTS	PIM
1979–80	Edmonton Oilers	79	51	86	137	21
1980–81	Edmonton Oilers	80	55	109	164	28
1981–82	Edmonton Oilers	80	92	120	212	26
1982–83	Edmonton Oilers	80	71	125	196	59
1983–84	Edmonton Oilers	74	87	118	205	39
1984–85	Edmonton Oilers	80	73	135	208	52
1985–86	Edmonton Oilers	80	52	163	215	46
1986–87	Edmonton Oilers	79	62	121	183	28
1987–88	Edmonton Oilers	64	40	109	149	24
1988–89	Los Angeles Kings	78	54	114	168	26
1989–90	Los Angeles Kings	73	40	102	142	42
1990–91	Los Angeles Kings	78	41	122	163	16
1991–92	Los Angeles Kings	74	31	90	121	34
1992–93	Los Angeles Kings	45	16	49	65	6
1993–94	Los Angeles Kings	81	38	92	130	20
1994–95	Los Angeles Kings	48	11	37	48	6
1995–96	Los Angeles Kings	62	15	66	81	32
1995–96	St. Louis Blues	18	8	13	21	2
1996–97	New York Rangers	82	25	72	97	28
1997–98	New York Rangers	82	23	67	90	28
1998–99	New York Rangers	70	9	53	62	14
NHL Totals		**1487**	**894**	**1963**	**2857**	**577**

PLAYOFFS

Season	Team	GP	G	A	PTS	PIM
1979–80	Edmonton Oilers	3	2	1	3	0
1980–81	Edmonton Oilers	9	7	14	21	4
1981–82	Edmonton Oilers	5	5	7	12	8
1982–83	Edmonton Oilers	16	12	26	38	4
1983–84	Edmonton Oilers	19	13	22	35	12
1984–85	Edmonton Oilers	18	17	30	47	4
1985–86	Edmonton Oilers	10	8	11	19	2
1986–87	Edmonton Oilers	21	5	29	34	6
1987–88	Edmonton Oilers	19	12	31	43	16
1988–89	Los Angeles Kings	11	5	17	22	0
1989–90	Los Angeles Kings	7	3	7	10	0
1990–91	Los Angeles Kings	12	4	11	15	2
1991–92	Los Angeles Kings	6	2	5	7	2
1992–93	Los Angeles Kings	24	15	25	40	4
1994–95	Los Angeles Kings	--	--	--	--	--
1994–95	Los Angeles Kings	--	--	--	--	--
1995–96	St. Louis Blues	13	2	14	16	0
1996–97	New York Rangers	15	10	10	20	2
1997–98	New York Rangers	--	--	--	--	--
1998–99	New York Rangers	--	--	--	--	--
NHL Totals		**208**	**122**	**260**	**382**	**66**

VINCENT LECAVALIER

THE STANLEY CUP
GOES SOUTH

There wasn't supposed to be a seventh game of the 2004 Stanley Cup Finals. The Calgary Flames were favoured to win the series on home ice during the sixth game, but an overtime goal by the Tampa Bay Lightning spoiled the party for all of Canada. Now, on the night of June 7, the Cup could find a home in Florida if the Lightning could come up with one more victory. Winning a seventh and deciding game is never easy, even on home ice, but the hometown crowd was ready to give their team a boost.

"Do it for Dave," read one sign held by a fan, a reference to Tampa Bay captain Dave Andreychuk and his quest for a championship for the first time in a 20-year NHL career. Another sign read "Vinny: Simply the Best." If it was meant to inspire centre Vincent Lecavalier, the fan who took the time to write need not have worried. Lecavalier, a

Lecavalier lifts the Cup after his 2004 Stanley Cup victory.

first overall selection by the Lightning in 1998 and clearly Tampa Bay's most talented player, was ready for this game. Earlier in the series, after a Tampa Bay victory, Lecavalier had said, "We know that Calgary is a hardworking team and they played very well but we have a lot of character. We're not questioning ourselves."

The Lightning opened the scoring with a goal by Ruslan Fedotenko when the Tampa winger put in a rebound past Calgary netminder Miikka Kiprusoff on a powerplay at 13:31 of the first period. The game stayed close until the 14:38 mark of the second period. Lecavalier dug the puck out of the corner and took it between two Flames defenders before spotting a wide open Fedotenko in the slot. Fedotenko snapped a shot past Kiprusoff to give Tampa a 2–0 lead as they went into the third period. Calgary pressed hard to get back into the game and scored a goal on a powerplay with just over ten minutes to go to make it 2–1. Backed by the excellent goaltending of Nikolai Khabibulin, the Lightning held off the hard-charging Flames and even survived a penalty with one minute left in the game. As the game ended, the crowd of over 22,700 began to celebrate.

When it was all done, Lecavalier reflected on the last few years in Tampa Bay playing with his good friend Brad Richards, who had just been awarded the Conn

Smythe Trophy as the best player in the playoffs. "This is unbelievable for both of us. We were in last place for four years when we first got here."

Lecavalier had probably played his best game of the playoffs, winning 13 faceoffs (only Andreychuk won more for the Lightning with 14) and tying for the team lead with three shots on net during the decisive match.

After many years of failure, it was a great moment of triumph for the player most people recognized as the face of the Tampa Bay franchise. At that moment, Lecavalier and his team were champions.

FROM QUEBEC TO SASKATCHEWAN . . . AND BACK

Vincent was the youngest of three children born to Yvon and Christine Lecavalier on April 21, 1980, in Île Bizard, Quebec, a suburb of Montreal. Yvon was an athletic man who had played junior hockey. Many of the traits he had for hockey were passed on to Vincent and to Philippe and Genevieve, Lecavalier's older siblings. Lecavalier began skating at the age of two and a half, and a toy hockey stick was always by his side as he toddled around the basement. Since Yvon worked mostly in the evenings, his daytime hours were free. After his father's afternoon nap, Lecavalier would be quick to tell his father it was time to go to the rink. While at the outdoor rinks, the weather could get bitterly cold, but Lecavalier could be sure that his father would be there to watch him. There were few other adults around, and his father could be seen jumping up and down at times just to stay warm.

Lecavalier during the 1998 Canadian Hockey League Top Prospects Game

Afterwards they would warm up back at home as they talked about hockey.

Lecavalier's father would sometimes rent ice time at a local rink in order to teach Vinny all about the game he had come to love. He would set up orange cones on the ice and Lecavalier would weave through them, learning to become more agile. All that practise led him to become so good that, at just four years old, he started to play organized hockey against boys who were eight or nine. Well trained in the rules and moves of hockey by his father, Lecavalier knew exactly where to line up for a faceoff and even understood the icing rule at such a young age. And Lecavalier was by no means overwhelmed by the older children. By the time he was six, he had become something of a local legend. Fans came out to see this young boy dominate the ice, and he was always expected to score. In one game, when Lecavalier failed to score in a game that had been much anticipated, Yvon gave his son such a lecture that Lecavalier began to cry. It was the last time Yvon would raise his voice to Vincent about hockey.

Lecavalier's father was committed to giving his son the best opportunity possible to make it in hockey. When he noticed that Lecavalier needed help with his skating stride, Yvon hired a figure skating coach. Lecavalier's talent on the ice was noticed by Notre Dame College prep school in Wilcox, Saskatchewan. It was well known as a great hockey school having developed NHL-calibre players like Wendel Clark, Gary Leeman, Russ Courtnall, Rod Brind'Amour and Curtis Joseph. The coach at Notre Dame was former Canadian National Team member Terry O'Malley. Since Lecavalier's brother Philippe had attended the school with some success, Vincent was anxious to go through the same program. O'Malley felt Lecavalier had great potential, but standing just 5'11" (1.8 metres) and considered small at just 155 pounds (70.3 kilograms), Lecavalier had some work to do to make it to college hockey.

The time spent in Saskatchewan proved to be a great investment. In his first year, Lecavalier not only grew two inches (five centimetres), he added bulk to his wiry frame. He also put on great displays of stickhandling and driving to the net. The following season, in the 1995–96 campaign, Lecavalier scored 52 goals and added 52 assists in just 22 games. Then the Rimouski Océanic of the Quebec Major Junior Hockey League selected Lecavalier fourth overall in the 1996 midget draft. The lure of playing so much closer to home was too strong for Lecavalier. He gave up his chance at a scholarship to an American college and left Notre Dame to join Rimouski for the next two seasons.

His performance for the Océanic drew comparisons to previous great French Canadian juniors like Jean Béliveau (Lecavalier wore sweater number four just like the former Montreal captain) and Mario Lemieux.

Lecavalier recorded 103 points in 1996–97 and topped that a year later with 115 points (44 goals and 71 assists). In the 1998 playoffs, he led all scorers with 41 points. His efforts were good, but the Océanic were beaten by Val d'Or in the league finals, keeping Lecavalier out of the Memorial Cup tournament. Still, his performance caught the eye of professional scouts. He was considered one of the best juniors available in the upcoming NHL Entry Draft. Little did he realize just how much pressure was about to be upon his young shoulders.

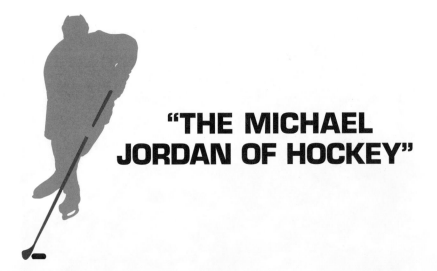

"THE MICHAEL JORDAN OF HOCKEY"

By the time Vincent was eligible for the NHL Entry Draft, he had grown to 6'3" (1.91 metres) and weighed 182 pounds (82.5 kilograms). Scouts were excited at the possibility of the 18-year-old joining their team. Although the San Jose Sharks won the draft lottery that year, the Tampa Bay Lightning had made a deal with them to get the first pick. The Lightning had been a deeply troubled organization since they started play as an expansion club in 1992–93 and had made just one playoff appearance, in 1995–96. Now they had another chance to put a fresh face on their team, and all signs pointed to Lecavalier being selected first overall.

Former NHL player Don Murdoch was the head scout of the Lightning, and he made it clear there was no doubt about who the Tampa Bay club was going to take. "The race for the top pick in the draft is over," he said. "Lecavalier is

Lecavalier pulls on a Tampa Bay Lightning jersey at the 1998 draft.

so far ahead of everybody else it's scary. He's an all-round player. He has size and strength. His hockey sense and skills are outstanding," Murdoch gushed.

Team owner Art Williams, a wealthy insurance executive from Birmingham, Alabama, got a little too excited. Before announcing Lecavalier as the first pick of the 1998 draft, he declared that the Lightning were drafting "the Michael Jordan of hockey," referring to one of the greatest basketball players of all time. Although flattering, it seemed a big declaration for a draft pick. And Williams didn't stop there. He added, "We're giving him a big, big, percentage of making the team this year. His talent is obvious. He is going to be a Hall-of-Famer, no question. The Lord has blessed him with a unique gift."

> *"To be number one overall is a great honour. I'm relieved everything is over."*

Lightning coach Jacques Demers (a man known for making outrageous statements himself at times) was not very pleased with the comments made by Williams. Demers knew what kind of pressure Lecavalier was going to face as the top choice, and didn't want his potential new superstar to face even more scrutiny. But it didn't seem to bother Lecavalier too much; he simply said that it was an honour to be selected first overall, and expressed relief the entire process was over. Soon afterwards, he signed a three-year contract with

Tampa Bay worth $975,000 in the first year, which was the maximum salary allowed for rookies. But it was estimated he could earn between $8 to $15 million if he met a series of performance bonus clauses and incentives. Williams was right about one thing — Lecavalier did make the team as an 18-year old-and, although he struggled, he managed to score 13 goals and total 28 points in 82 games, playing mostly on Tampa's third line. The Lightning were still a terrible team, winning only 17 games that season. The next season Lecavalier tried even harder to help the team and scored 25 goals for a total of 67 points in 80 games. In spite of Vincent's better performance, the Lightning won only 19 games. It was going to be a long road to the top of the NHL for Tampa Bay.

Ownership and coaching changes didn't help the Lightning much, and the team floundered. However, one coach saw more in Lecavalier than anyone else. When the Lightning traded captain Chris Gratton to Buffalo, head coach Steve Ludzik named Lecavalier as the new team leader. At just 19 years old, he became the second-youngest captain in NHL history. But this didn't worry Ludzik: he saw a work ethic he liked and a maturity off the ice which showed that Vinny could be a good leader.

That year, Lecavalier showed a good example to his teammates by reporting to camp in good shape. And he always tried to find a way to encourage his teammates, even when they felt they were struggling. But Tampa Bay was struggling as a team, and it wasn't anything Lecavalier could fix. Then, in 2000–01, Ludzik was fired and replaced by no-nonsense John Torterella, who wasn't so keen on having a such a young captain. To make matters worse for Vincent, the next two seasons his point production fell (51 and 37 points respectively). After the 2000–01 season, Tortorella decided to strip Lecavalier of his captaincy. It was clear Lecavalier was going to have to refocus and just concentrate on playing hockey. The good news was that the Lightning were putting together a very good team . . . even though Lecavalier was almost traded away.

LIGHTNING STRIKES
TAMPA BAY

Tortorella and Lecavalier did *not* see eye to eye.

Tortorella thought that the team's biggest star was a lazy player. They seemed to be constantly clashing. The team's general manager, Rick Dudley, stood behind his coach. He even tried to trade the slick centre. A deal was all but finalized that would have sent Vincent to the Toronto Maple Leafs. But then, as was common as the team tried to rebuild, Dudley was let go and replaced by the unknown Jay Feaster. The new general manager brought Lecavalier and Tortorella into a meeting and told them they had to find a way to work together. "I don't want to be known as the general manager who traded away Vinny Lecavalier," he said.

The discussion seemed to reassure Lecavalier, and he responded with a 78-point (33 goals, 45 assists) season in 2002–03. The Lightning made the playoffs for just the second time in their history, and even won one round. But the next season would prove to be the most memorable for Lecavalier and his teammates.

In 2003–04, Lecavalier was a key to the team's success as the Lightning won a club record of 46 games for a total of 106 points, finishing first in the NHL's Southeast Division. Lecavalier scored 32 times and added 34 assists during the regular season, but he had plenty of help in producing offence: teammates Martin St. Louis (winner of the Art Ross Trophy that year for the scoring title), Cory Stillman and Brad Richards were all in the top ten of league scoring. The team also had a strong checking line led by Tim Taylor and Lightning captain Dave Andreychuk, an NHL veteran who helped Lecavalier throughout his games. Tampa Bay had everything needed to go a long way in the playoffs.

"Every time you step up [to a new level], play gets a little faster; the players are bigger and more skilled. You have to make changes and adjust."

In the first round of the playoffs, the New York Islanders were no match for the Lightning, who won in just five games. The second round of the playoffs was a little emotional for Lecavalier, who played against his hometown team, the Montreal Canadiens. However, he scored perhaps the biggest goal of the series in game three when he tied the game to make it 3–3 with just 17 seconds to play in regulation time.

Richards then scored the overtime winner, and Tampa went on to sweep the Habs in four straight games.

The Eastern Conference final against the Philadelphia Flyers was much harder, given the opposition. It went the full seven games, but once again, the Lightning prevailed on home ice with a 2–1 win.

The victory sent Tampa Bay to the Stanley Cup Finals for the first time in team history, and it was a long, hard-fought series before the Lightning eked out a 2–1 win in the seventh game to become champions. When Lecavalier stepped up to Calgary's captain Jarome Iginla during a confrontation, it surprised many. It also inspired his teammates.

Sharing the Stanley Cup victory with centre Brad Richards was especially gratifying for Lecavalier. They had both attended Notre Dame College in Saskatchewan and were teammates in Quebec. Richards was even chosen in the same draft, selected 64th overall in 1998. The two players became key components of the Lightning's Stanley Cup win. Richards led all playoff scorers with 26 points in 23 games and earned the first Conn Smythe Trophy for

"Each game he played in the playoffs, he went to another level. Vincent's an incredible talent. It's one thing to be talented, but if you don't work hard, it's worth nothing. He works extremely hard."
— Wayne Gretzky

Lecavalier on tour with his The Cup in Montreal

the Tampa Bay club. Both players had struggled for many years, but winning the championship confirmed their star status and they revelled in sharing the moment.

The Lightning looked forward to defending their championship during the 2004–05 season but there was something else for some members of the team to do before embarking on another long NHL season.

VINNY AT THE WORLD CUP

Vincent Lecavalier had represented Canada during international hockey tournaments, starting with the under-18 tournament in August of 1997. In one memorable game, the Canadians were down 2–0 to host nation the Czech Republic going into the third period. Lecavalier turned it on and set up Canada's first goal, then scored the winner for a 3–2 victory. He also played for Canada a year later in the 1998 world junior tournament in Helsinki, Finland, but Canada finished a disappointing eighth in the ten-team tourney.

In September 2004, Canada was putting together a team for the second World Cup of Hockey. Brad Richards and Martin St. Louis were selected for Team Canada, but surprisingly, a spot wasn't offered to Lecavalier. However, when Steve Yzerman was injured, Team Canada's executive director, Wayne Gretzky, added Lecavalier to the Canadian

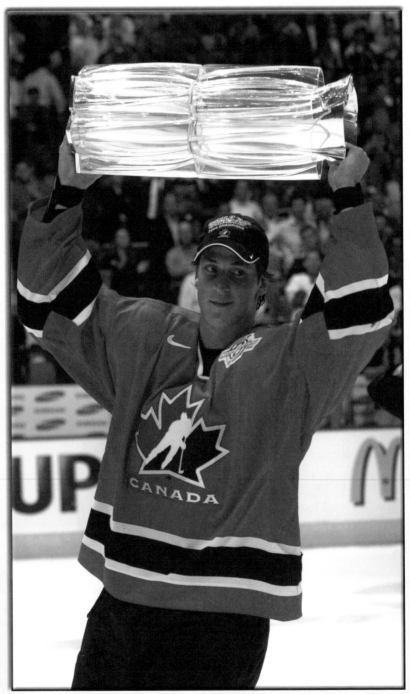

Lecavalier hoists the World Cup trophy.

roster. Elated at being added to the team, Lecavalier arrived in great shape. He earned a spot in the starting lineup and, in six games, produced two goals (one an overtime winner against the Czech Republic that sent Canada to the final against Finland) and five assists — only Lightning teammate Fredrik Modin had more points with eight for the Swedish team. Canada won the World Cup and Lecavalier was named the Most Valuable Player of the tournament, edging out Canadian netminder Martin Brodeur.

Gretzky was impressed by what he saw from Lecavalier. "He works extremely hard. If you watch him closely when he loses the puck, he doesn't go for a skate, he stops on a dime and goes back to get it. . . . He is going to be part of Team Canada for a lot of years to come." (Gretzky was correct, as Lecavalier was later named to Team Canada for the 2006 Winter Olympics.)

> "He's like Jean Béliveau. He's even got the same number."
>
> —Former Edmonton Oilers director of player personnel Kevin Prendergast

With a Stanley Cup and World Cup now a part of his history, Lecavalier looked forward to becoming a more dominant force in the NHL. However, there was no season in 2004–05 due to a disagreement between the NHL players and team owners. Both Lecavalier and Richards went to play in Russia in order to stay sharp. The following season, after a settlement was reached, the

NHL was relaunched for the 2005–06 season with a focus on offence. Lecavalier produced a career-high 35 goals and totalled 75 points in 80 games. But the Lightning were knocked out of the playoffs in the first round.

Lecavalier played his greatest hockey the next season. During the 2006–07 campaign, he scored 52 times — the most of any player that season — and for the first time, he recorded over 100 points. Lecavalier's 108 point total was just behind Sidney Crosby (120) and Joe Thornton (114). Now up to 6'4" (1.93 metres) and 219 pounds (99 kilograms), Lecavalier was not only good on the attack, he was also a top defensive player. He strived to be a complete player who competed consistently every night. His stellar performance earned him a place on the second All-Star Team — the only time he had made one of the NHL's post-season teams thus far.

Lecavalier was being praised by many in hockey, including his ex-coach John Tortorella, who called his former player, "the best in the league" — something that he would never have said just a few years before. Tortorella was excited that Lecavalier had matured to earn such great respect.

"If he played in a major market, or . . . in Canada, they'd be building monuments in his honour," added Lightning general manager Jay Feaster. "That's how good he is. It's just unfortunate that not everybody seems to know that.

. . . somewhere along the line the hype machine and the media have forgotten just how good number 4 is."

The superstar player had also taken $3 million of his own money and given it to a local hospital that was under construction, making Lecavalier even more of a hero in the Tampa area.

Lecavalier may not have become "the Michael Jordan of hockey," but he certainly was something special.

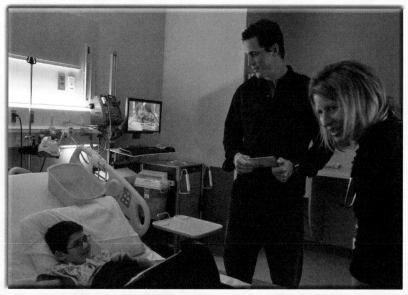

Lecavalier visits the All Children's Hospital in St. Petersburg, Florida.

THE FUTURE

In 2007–08, Lecavalier was given back the captaincy and recorded a 92-point season (including 40 goals), despite the team finishing last overall with just 31 wins and 71 points. During the 2008 draft, the Lightning selected first overall. They took Steven Stamkos with the pick, a highly skilled player they hoped to build around, much as they had years ago with Lecavalier.

Lecavalier himself was playing out a contract that was paying him millions of dollars a year. The Lightning organization was happy enough to pay their top performer and needed to re-sign their franchise player. Perfectly content to play out his career in Tampa Bay, Lecavalier signed an 11-year deal which would pay him a total of $85 million. As soon as he agreed to the deal, rumours started to swirl that the Lightning's newest owners would never be able to afford the contract and would most likely try to trade the star centre. Montreal was the team most often mentioned as a possible destination for Lecavalier, and the Canadiens fans loved the idea of a local hero coming home to put on the famous red, white and blue sweater. The lure of the Canadiens securing a French-Canadian star was too much to resist but Montreal general manager Bob Gainey was unable to reach an agreement with the Lightning. Lecavalier spent the 2008–09 season in Tampa Bay and produced 67 points (29 goals, 38 assists) in 77 games before a wrist injury ended his season with just five games left.

The Tampa Bay franchise nearly reverted to its earlier, terrible days: the team missed the 2008–09 playoffs and recorded only 24 wins (the second-worst record in the league that season). There were new people in management, including Brian Lawton as general manager and Rick Tocchet as head coach. Many of the players Lecavalier had won the Stanley Cup with in 2004, including Brad Richards, had moved to other teams. Today, the only two remaining are Lecavalier and Martin St. Louis, and it appears that even their time in Florida may soon be coming to an end.

Unfortunately, Lecavalier got off to a poor start in the 2009–10 season, and as a result wasn't chosen for Team Canada's appearance at the 2010 Winter Olympic Games in Vancouver. But as the season moved along, he improved and finished with 24 goals and 46 assists, although the

Lightning missed the playoffs again. The numbers added to Lecavalier's career totals as Tampa Bay's all-time leader in goals scored (326), most assists (413), most points (739) and most games played (869). Lecavalier's contract and his star status in Tampa Bay may make it difficult to move him to another team, but he has proven himself to be a great NHL player, and certainly the best player in franchise history for the Lightning.

Lecavalier battles it out in the corner with Patrice Bergeron of the Boston Bruins.

VINCENT LECAVALIER

Born: April 21, 1980, in Île Bizard, Quebec

Height: 6 ft 4 in (1.93 m)

Weight: 223 lb (101 kg)

Position: Centre

Shot: Left

Pro clubs: Tampa Bay Lightning

Playing career: 1998–present

REGULAR SEASON

Season	Team	GP	G	A	PTS	PIM
1998–99	Tampa Bay Lightning	82	13	15	28	23
1999–00	Tampa Bay Lightning	80	25	42	67	43
2000–01	Tampa Bay Lightning	68	23	28	51	66
2001–02	Tampa Bay Lightning	76	20	17	37	61
2002–03	Tampa Bay Lightning	80	33	45	78	39
2003–04	Tampa Bay Lightning	81	32	34	66	52
2005–06	Tampa Bay Lightning	80	35	40	75	90
2006–07	Tampa Bay Lightning	82	52	56	108	44
2007–08	Tampa Bay Lightning	81	40	52	92	89
2008–09	Tampa Bay Lightning	77	29	38	67	54
2009–10	Tampa Bay Lightning	82	24	46	70	63
NHL Totals		**869**	**326**	**413**	**739**	**624**

PLAYOFFS

Season	Team	GP	G	A	PTS	PIM
1998–99	Tampa Bay Lightning	--	--	--	--	--
1999–00	Tampa Bay Lightning	--	--	--	--	--
2000–01	Tampa Bay Lightning	--	--	--	--	--
2001–02	Tampa Bay Lightning	--	--	--	--	--
2002–03	Tampa Bay Lightning	11	3	3	6	22
2003–04	Tampa Bay Lightning	23	9	7	16	25
2005–06	Tampa Bay Lightning	5	1	3	4	7
2006–07	Tampa Bay Lightning	6	5	2	7	10
2007–08	Tampa Bay Lightning	--	--	--	--	--
2008–09	Tampa Bay Lightning	--	--	--	--	--
2009–10	Tampa Bay Lightning	--	--	--	--	--
NHL Totals		**45**	**18**	**15**	**33**	**64**

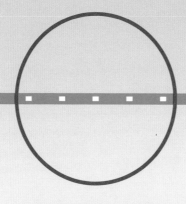

INDEX